Dedicated in the

Memory of

My beloved wife Sheela

LOVE
AND
DIVORCE

MARRIAGE SWOT
WITH 69 i-QUOTES

MUTHYA VENKATESH

Contents

Preface

It was the month of April 2021 the entire world was gripped in the deadly pandemic wave of Corona virus, suddenly on a Sunday early morning my wife screamed at me asking why did you get up so early? I rubbed my eyes and saw it was still dark and when I checked the time on my phone it was 3.36 am, and nobody was around me; I must have been dreaming.

It was exactly a week back when my beloved wife fell prey to the new variant of the Corona virus and within 48 hours she departed to heaven leaving all of us shocked and my thirty years of happy married life was shattered within 30 hours.

Gradually within a few months I started getting out of grief and managed to accept the harsh reality of leading life without a spouse.

Life is very unpredictable; every day the sun which rises must set in the evening and in this process, it takes us one day closer to death. Every living being born on this planet must die one day and there is no exception, what remains back is memories in various forms.

GOD has created everything in pairs to balance the nature and for the survival and existence of living beings which include male and female for the purpose of reproduction. As the civilization grew with arrival of various cultures and religious beliefs the concept of marriage has taken birth to legitamize the social relationship between a man and woman.

Marriage in India is a sacred ritual which is performed in the presence of relatives and friends with an intention that the married couple lead a blissful life.

Over the decades the way marriages are performed has undergone a lot of changes based on generational evolution, but the core objective remained same.

During the last couple of decades, the longevity of marriage has started reducing, men and women have started parting away which gave birth to a new syndrome called Divorce.

I have spent 30 years of happy married life with my wife and even now I cherish each day spent with her. There was nothing common between us, we were poles apart in all aspects, but still we fell in love and had a great married life.

My wife was my best friend and foe; there were absolutely no secrets hidden between us, even the smallest good or bad thing we shared between us, which in some instances were totally irrelevant, but since we cultivated the habit of not hiding anything between us, we used to share. There were lot of issues on which we used to argue like archrivals, but at the end based on the result or the outcome of the actions/situation the loser would accept the defeat and forget the argument. On complex issues there used to be healthy discussion and even if a solo decision was taken which later proved wrong, there was no hesitation from either side to accept the fault. The biggest secret of our marriage was from day one "we agreed to disagree".

My wife and I were both from an ordinary middle-class family without any strong educational background and when I got married, I had a minimum bank balance, and neither of us had any ancestral property nor financial support to start our married life. We made a very small beginning during which my wife also worked for about two years till the birth of our first child. During this point we both took a major decision, wherein my wife decided that she would take care of kids and family, and earning money was my sole responsibility. The first half of married life was a smooth journey, but after the birth of my second child who was born with physical disability my financial requirements shot up, added to that I had to take care of my aged parent and also had to give a good education to my elder son. The physical and financial hardships which me and my wife had undergone during second half of our married life is just unimaginable, but due to our unwavering faith in GOD, helped us to survive. Even during the worst crisis when I used to struggle to run the family daily, my wife never lost trust in me, and every night we used to have a joyful dinner. Just before the covid pandemic I lost my second child after battling against all odds for 17 long years. My wife sacrificed and dedicated her whole life for the sake of the family. My relatives, friends, colleagues, whoever had met her just once, always remember and wonder how she could handle so much pressure with a relaxed smile on her face.

After the death of my wife every day I recollect the memorable days spent in her company and in the process when I started analyzing how we could live so happily, when the present generation young couples are losing interest in their spouses with in few years and for small issues they are breaking away; this thought has really surprised me and forced to introspect the success of my marriage.

Wedding event has become a lucrative business in India and millions of people survive on this, but unfortunately the stars of the event, the beautiful young couple when they come out of the extravaganza and honeymoon trips, start understanding the marriage consequences.

Marriage in my opinion is a simple ceremony that has become a complex subject for the present generation, hence I thought of sharing my views and opinions which are based on my marriage experience and after studying more than hundred married couples' lifestyle across caste and religion.

Marriages are not made in heaven, but it is a bonding of two beautiful souls who create a wonderful world for two different families.

I consider my effort in bringing out this book worthwhile if more marriages are successful.

I would like to thank my son Karan and daughter-in-law Ragini for their support in writing this book.

Part A

Chapter 1

Marriage – A "Knotty" Affair

Marriage is not an institution but a social contract between two people, in which a man and a woman are socially permitted to live together without losing their status in the community. Marriage is not merely concerned with the couple; rather it affects the whole society and future generations. In Hindu view, marriage is not a concession to human weakness, but a means for spiritual growth. People are soul mates who, through the institution of marriage, can direct the energy associated with their individual instincts and passion into the progress of their souls.

Marriage has played an important role in the Indian society across all segments of people, starting from the ancient Indian royals' families to the present generation business class who use this occasion to expand their reach to new regions.

The oldest marriage alliance making process which even now exists in middle class and rural families is parents selecting the match for their son or daughter based on their religion and caste parameters, which has been largely successful till the early 21st century.

In the new era of technology and competitive world, the general family lifestyle has undergone a lot of changes and moved away from the traditional practices. In the 20th century, the main responsibility of woman was to manage house and family, money making job was the sole responsibility of the men in the family; but with the changing times and rise of inflation it has become necessary for the middle-class woman to share the financial responsibility. This change has become an important part of marriage alliance process wherein both man and woman take decisions based on each other financial capability.

There is another segment of the new generation of people influenced by western culture, who question the need for marriage for biological needs and believe in pure materialistic bonding and pleasures. The core problem in the present fast-paced competitive environment where people have become less emotional and more logical are unable to understand the true value and benefits of matrimony relationship. Emotion and logic never go together, relationships are emotional bonding, and the success of marriage can never be defined in logical terms.

Some people question "is marriage a necessity"?

Yes, as per Hindu religion it's one of the few mandatory rituals a person must perform in his life span between birth and death. Some people opt to stay as a bachelor whole life, but in Hindu religion lots of rituals can be performed only by husband and wife, and salvation after death can be achieved only when children perform the final rites and rituals.

From the human psychological perspective, the best way to overcome professional stress and have a stable mindset is by sharing life with a partner, which in turn may find solutions for complex personal issues.

Most people enter wedlock because of sheer pressure from parents and family members, without trying to understand the purpose of marriage. There is another category of people who get attracted to a girl or boy and for the sake of living together they get married, assuming both love each other and without thinking about future paternal and family-building relationship complications.

Marriage is a lifelong commitment between two people, but unfortunately most people don't think about this aspect and get married with a short-term vision and objective driven by desire or compulsion, and in the process, they make wrong choices in selecting their life partner.

The most important aspect for a successful marriage is to select the right partner, which is the most difficult task, even in the current internet era wherein hundreds of matrimonial portals are flooded with lots of personal data of marriage seekers.

One of the key factors which plays a major role in partner selection is when the marriage seekers have a clear view on the profile of their proposed life partner requirements. Normally when parents look for an alliance for their children, they focus mostly on religion, language and financial stability of the prospective bride/groom and don't really try to explore if the characters of boy and girl can get along without trouble after marriage. Before selecting a life partner, first decide what type of husband or wife you want and next if the same person can be a good mother or father to your child and after getting satisfied with these two issues you can look for your other parameters. Remember nobody is made for each other, both need to work for each other to become a perfect couple.

If we study and understand the following Hindu marriage rituals it clearly shows the path for happy married life.

A) One of the most important aspects in Hindu marriage is tying of "Mangalasutra". The literal meaning of Mangalasutra if translated in English is Happy Principle, which is tied with three knots around bride's neck by the groom.

The importance of mangalasutra : A mangalasutra symbolizes the union of two souls and their love for each other and promise to stay together. It is also said to protect the couple from negativity.

Some people also debate why Mangalasutra is tied only to girls, and after marriage why they only must go and stay with boys' families. In Hindu culture, girl is the symbol of happiness and wealth, hence for a prosperous relationship and expansion of family she is welcomed by bridegroom side.

B) Another very interesting ritual which precedes the mangalasutra process is when the bride & groom both stand face to face with a curtain between them and after chanting a few mantras when this curtain is removed both keep their hands on each other's head which is a symbolic pledge not to hide anything between them after getting into wed lock.

If the Hindu marriage rituals are understood and followed correctly it leads to happy married life.

Marriage is not like a three-hour cinema movie, but it's like a web series with lots of new episodes and seasons with unexpected twists and turns. The first season of marriage is always very beautiful since it involves the glittery wedding rituals and celebrations followed by honeymoon trips which are usually spread over one to two years.

The second season starts with family expansion with the arrival of kids, which really starts putting pressure on both wife and husband, and at these points the involvement of parents and in-laws becomes necessary which may gradually reduce the romantic relationship between husband and wife as they become more involved as father and mother.

Another important aspect is the individual attitude towards lifestyle after marriage, wherein some people don't like to change their bachelor life habits after marriage, which is not a good approach towards married life. A daughter/son becomes wife & husband, mother & father after marriage and everyone needs to adapt to the situation and act responsibly for the family's success.

The critical phase in a marriage is between three to ten years, when the family expands, which increases the financial requirements along with increased work pressure at home, for which lots of patience and understanding is required between the couple, without which life becomes very miserable. If there are no kids a different kind of pressure is built by family members and relatives which may affect husband and wife relationships, but usually children play a very important role in keeping the family united.

The third and fourth seasons of marriage are from 11th to 30th years when the children cross the teen age and the role of parents becomes very important in shaping their future, and in this phase of life one of the spouse must take extra responsibility towards family.

Family and profession are both equally important, but most people think career means professional growth in their respective fields of interest like sports, music, arts, culture etc., and the most common area is business and office work where they spend long hours at the expense of their family life to achieve their goals.

Unfortunately, most people don't consider family happiness as one of their career objectives and get along with blind belief that earning more money will automatically bring happiness and success in the family.

The success formula which is discussed across all segments of business and other events is "teamwork".   Teamwork does not mean every member of the team doing the same task simultaneously, but everyone is doing their allocated responsibility in coordination with other members of the team for success of their team goal. Similarly, after marriage, wife and husband should distribute the family responsibilities between them which will enable both to find enough time for enjoying married life and building a strong relationship.

There is a misconception in the present generation couples that both husband and wife should be financially independent for the success of the marriage since it gives both of them self-confidences to handle themselves individually in case of marriage break up. This is the most negative mindset to start a marriage relationship, since the main purpose of having a partner is to share your life with each other in good or bad times. Financial stability in marriage is very important, but it does not mean both wife and husband should slog throughout the day to only earn money. In first few years of marriage it may be required for both couple to work for money since they have to set up a family, but after 5,10 years when the kids start growing up, one of them has to take the responsibility of the managing the house/family, but unfortunately this is not an easy task and it may lead to tension in the relationship between husband and wife.

Good things don't come easily, and marriage is a precious gift which needs to be handled and preserved carefully. To unfold the "knotty" marriage and make it happy and long-lasting , it's very important to follow the SWOT formula.

Chapter – II

Marriage SWOT

Like in business it is very important to follow the SWOT formula in marriage also. What is SWOT in marriage?

- SUPPORT
- WORK
- OWNERSHIP
- TRUST

SUPPORT

The definition of support is:

- To agree and give encouragement to someone or something because you want him, or her to succeed
- To say yes to suggestion or an idea

- To help someone emotionally or in a practical way

- To support an activity, hobby etc.

For a marriage to sustain and last for long periods of time, support plays an important role in bringing both partners to workable situations in life.

People enter marriage when they feel the need to have a life partner with whom they can share their individual goal and jointly work towards achieving their life ambitions which keeps on changing when they add more members to their family. Because of physical attraction and intimacy, the initial couple of years in marriage passes away without many hurdles or troubles, but the law of diminishing interest in conflicting zones catches up sooner or later which opens the pandora box of uncertainty.

It is common for any human being to experience stress and perform the routine daily tasks with consistent efficiency for long periods of time without intermittent breaks, and when this does not happen sparks start flying and can lead to losing interest in tasks or people associated within that zone.

The most adapted practice in Indian society is that after marriage the girl must leave her parent house and stay in the boy's house in an alien environment. In India the lifestyle, and food habits differ from house to house even in the same religion or caste with common spoken language.

The transformation of a woman starts immediately after marriage when she becomes a wife & daughter-in-law and must live with a new group of people which may be a challenging task if there is no cooperation from all the family members, especially the complete support of husband which is very critical for the success of marriage.

The role of husband (in support of wife):

The most important job is to make the wife feel comfortable in his house and help her develop a rapport with other family members by informing her about their household practices, which can be done in a phased manner as and when the situation arises, but without giving surprises.

No individual would like to be confronted in their private space zone by a stranger, hence it takes time for people to understand each other because of which small differences in opinions or practices may crop up which need to be handled carefully by the husband since it is his responsibility to ensure that there is a harmonious bonding between his wife and other family members.

Adapting to new environment and changing routine lifestyles to suit the same cannot happen over a summer or monsoon, it takes time; like it's not possible to live at home the hostel style of life, which is even more tough for woman since after marriage she will have the additional responsibility of an extended family.

The most important and difficult task is feeding the family members, since before marriage cooking is not a routine activity for girls or boys as it's taken care by their mothers, but after marriage when the wife has to cook for whole family it will not be an easy task; the husband needs to extend helping hand along with convincing his family members to adjust with his wife cooking style until she get a clarity on their taste buds.

Every girl has a lot of dreams and expectations from a married life, and since she has moved to husband's house it is his responsibility to understand her requirements and try to realize her dreams to a possible extent without hurting the sentiments of other family members.

It is not easy for girls to keep distance from parents immediately after marriage, whether a husband likes it or not, he should not interfere in his wife's relationship with her parents or family members after marriage and she should be given full freedom to take any decisions concerned with her family matters.

Women are creators hence their metabolism is different from men; this should be understood by the husbands during their physical relationship. Women undergo lots of stress and their moods fluctuate during their monthly periods, which may reflect in their actions. Husbands who really love their wives should understand this and give lot of emotional support and try to reduce their workload and give her rest as much as possible.

The most challenging phase for a woman is transforming from a wife to mother, which starts from pregnancy and continues till the end…. Nobody understands a woman's pregnancy problems during gestation period better than a woman, hence it would be a good option if she is under her mother's guidance for couple of months before and after childbirth. The husband needs to provide emotional support and ensure the family environment is not disturbed due to her absence.

(Authors note: I have seen my child's birth in front of my eyes, it's just because the Doctor was very impressed with the way I have taken care of my wife during pregnancy, in fact every time I took her for monthly check up, the Doctor used to tell my wife, "by looking at your husband I can tell you everything is perfect and you will have normal delivery" and on the day after my wife was taken to delivery ward, within few minutes a nurse came and took me to the ward wherein I saw my wife was very relaxed, which the Doctor wanted to show me and felt my presence would be even more beneficial. To be honest at the time of childbirth I was cracking joke on which both my wife and Doctor were laughing, and later the nurses in the ward told me they had never seen such a joyful environment in the delivery ward. After about 25 years once I met the same Doctor at an airport and she remembered me and told "I have done thousands of deliveries, but I have never seen a couple like you". Even after childbirth within a couple of weeks my wife was back from her parents' house, because she felt that I can take care of her better than anyone.)

Children play a crucial role in the second half of married life because of their responsibility husband and wife must sort out their differences and support each other for the bright future of the kids.

The role of wife (in support of husband):

Men generally don't express their feelings directly instead go into silent mode, which makes it very difficult for opposite person to understand their reactions. Girls discuss most of their issues with their mothers and continue the same after marriage also, but the relationship between a father and son is quite different and limited conversation happens between them, hence boys hardly discuss their personal issues with parents, and even if they do it will be mostly with their mother.

After marriage most of the wives expect the husbands to talk more with them and less with their parents, because of this whatever little close relationship he has with his parents starts drifting away. The husband must do a very tough balancing act between wife and parents, which takes a toll on his individual decision and actions.

Most boys grow up flirting with different people or things, and over a period they get addicted to some of them, which may not be easy to leave even after matured married life. Addiction can be cured by intoxication, but most of the time it happens the reverse way, people get addicted because of intoxication. Old habits die hard, especially when a person gets addicted to alcohol and smoking, it becomes a catalyst during stress and problems which sometimes may become a major issue after marriage. Love is stronger than anything else, and woman has the power to change, hence a caring husband will always adhere to his wife's wishes.

Unlike a wife, a husband rarely discusses his personal or marital problems with family members, and hence wife must try and dig into his personal issues and extend unconditional emotional support to help him overcome the problems.

In the present competitive environment office pressure leads to a lot of stress and in the event of losing a job by husband it may upset the family life, and the role of the wife becomes very important, as she must motivate and encourage him to be positive and not affect their relationship. Men can tolerate anything but would not like to be seen as insulted by or in front of women, hence an understanding life partner can easily help him sail over the tough period.

Friends are friends, good and bad among them are based on individual perception; for men it is very difficult to keep them away even after marriage, hence wives should try and avoid entering their husband's friendship zone unless it converts into family relationship.

The relationship between a husband and wife should be like a mirror and a person. Mirror never lies, it shows a person's true image, similarly a husband and wife should be reflection of each other's image.

WORK

Any living being on this planet needs to do something for survival and in human society the most used word for such action is called Work. Anything and everything a person can do can be labeled as work and can be classified under various categories.

For a successful happy married life also, it's very important to work hard to maintain a harmonious relationship between wife and husband along with other family members.

Responsibilities increase after marriage and unlike office jobs it does not have fixed working hours it's a 24/365 job with lots of unexpected and emergency work cropping up which can disrupt regular routine jobs.

To maintain and run a family in the present generation it's imperative for most husbands and wives to take up professional jobs to meet the ever-growing family expenses. The toughest job is managing office and homework which can easily bring rift between couples if not handled properly. The golden rule is Never bring office to home nor take home to office, if this rule can be successfully implemented half the problems are solved.

But unfortunately due to the impact of Covid pandemic work from home has become the norm of the day, which is like a double side sword hanging on married couples. There is an old saying if husband and wife keeping looking at each other for more than 12 hours a day, after few months they gradually start losing interest in each other, may be because they start observing each others small irrelevant mistakes also. But the main reason is when at office on a bad day when things go wrong you can shout at others or share problems with colleagues which may give you some relief, but at home you need to take the pressure within your selves and when it goes out of control you may shout at your spouse and if this repeats frequently it will develop cracks in your marriage. On the positive side if both couples really love and care of each other WFH can make married life more beautiful. (*Auther's note: Even before the pandemic for more than 10 years during the tough and critical phase of my married life, I used to work from home, because of which I used to support my wife when she was overload with work because of various factors, which is one of the reasons for our successful marriage*)

It is not possible for husband and wife to share their office work, but they can easily plan and share their homework so that one person is not overloaded, and to make this happen there should be mutual understanding between them, and this is where true love and concern for each other matters.

The critical phase in married life is when the work load inreases after the birth of children and the intensity of the pressure may stretch on up to ten years or even more. During this period, it's very important for the wife and husband to share the workload daily, if not done properly it may put huge pressure on one individual and may lead to regular conflicts and in the process the children's upbringing may be affected. Ideally after the birth of children to give the kids hygienic care with nutritional food, one of the couples should take a break from office jobs for a minimum of five years, which also ensures a strong emotional bonding with the parents.

No work is labelled as Woman's or Man's work, all works can be shared between the couple to ensure none of them individually are overburdened.

The family that works together stays together.

OWNERSHIP

People claim ownership of everything including those where their contribution or whatsoever is absolutely zero, yet they want to take credit for its existence.

Marriage is one of the most important events in life, for which people spend huge amounts of money and time entering the wedlock but never decide who takes the ownership for maintaining and sustaining a successful marriage.

Marriage is a joint ownership company wherein both wife and husband have equal share of responsibility, but in most cases neither of them have clarity on who must do what.

In the Indian marriage institution traditionally certain roles and responsibilities are associated with male and female; a newly married couple start life assuming each one of them is aware of their roles, and normally it does not affect daily routine life for couple of months or years, until the dual pressure of office and homework increases.

Sheer work pressure rages temper on frivolous issues and can lead to heated arguments which may go out of control and make it difficult for either of the couple to think beyond the current issue or the real reason for the difference of opinion.

Family is like a mini shopping mall which has all categories of products and services, but managed with a couple of people, hence it's important for each person to share the responsibility and ownership of all activities to ensure the family company runs smoothly.

The traditional Indian family system wherein men are responsible for income generation and women manage the finance and home is the best formula for a happy and successful marriage. Unfortunately, in the present generation there is a misconception among women, where in they feel let down and not treated equally with men when they are not allowed to compete with them in every area.

Life has become very competitive, everyone irrespective of sex, caste, religion etc., need to compete from childhood and it continues in different aspects literally till a person is alive. But family is like a cricket team, you need to have specialist batsmen, bowlers, wicket keeper and allrounders, then only you can perform well.   Similarly in family also you need to share responsibility and take ownership, especially when it comes to children's education, career etc.   There is no rule that only a husband must earn money and wife's job is running family, it can always be swapped based on mutual consent and convenience.   But there should never be competition between wife and husband.   No married life can be happy and successful for longer periods without a little bit of sacrifice from husband and wife. After marriage for husband wife is first, and for wife husband is first, but after children for both family should be first, then only life becomes easy and enjoyable.

TRUST

Trust is the most important ingredient in building long-term relationships between a husband and wife. Trust is as fragile as glass which can be easily broken by small stones of doubt, hence it's very important that husband and wife should not hide any secrets between them, because even a small drop of doubt if kept in cold storage for long time can become hard as ice and break the shield of trust.

Breach of trust is one of the major reasons for marriage break ups, though the issue may be very small, but keeping it secret by either partner and disclosing later may erupt with bundles of doubts and create immediate impact on the trust factor which may potentially break up the relationship if repeated.

Marriage is not an entertainment event, it's like a movie trailer which shows only the best scenes, but the final movie can be very successful or total flop; similarly married life can be very boring after few years, since you need to see the same faces every day but remember the famous quote "Known devil is better than unknown angel". There is no limit for expectation and nothing in this world is perfect for everyone, adjustment and compromise are part of life, and marriage is no exception. Successful marriage does not happen, you need to make it and keep on making it.

Part B

Divorce

Divorce is not the end of an error, but the beginning of a new problem. If you are caught between devil and deep sea, devil would be better option because there may be a possibility of negotiation.

People who dream of being independent for the whole of their life should never marry, because marriage is a commitment between two people to share their life, but not an experimental lab to decide which chemistry formula works better with different partners. From childhood till completion of education a person is under the guidance of parents and teachers, after that in professional career under peer pressure, finally after marriage person thinks he got his independence and can lead life as per his choice without taking instructions from anyone, but forgets the married partner also thinks the same way and purpose of marriage is lost if they cannot share life together. Long lasting bonding between two people does not happen over a few months, it's like a chunk of charcoal which if handled exceptionally well under pressure turns into diamond or burns into ashes.

Marriage is like a fragile thin glass which can be broken doubts & mistrust.

Divorce happens because of:

- DISREGARD
- INTEGRITY
- VULNERABILITY
- OCCUPATION
- RELATIONSHIP
- CHARACTER
- EGO

DISREGARD

Relationships break because of ego, disloyalty & disregard; until these habits are killed it would be foolish to expect long lasting love and trustworthy relationship between a husband and wife. Never ever neglect your spouse's feelings even if it sounds childish, because each person has a different way of expressing their feelings and you need to react cautiously, as nobody likes to be ignored by their partners.

Men and women are two different types of breeds and their thought process especially in relationship and family matters may be quite opposite, hence each other viewpoint and actions should be respected by both partners.

After marriage it would not be easy for either partner to immediately build a cordial relationship with their friends and family members, since it takes time for each of them to first accept their way of lifestyles, and after successfully sorting out the differences it may be possible to develop healthy relationships with other members. But in either case both the partners should never disregard family members or close friends, and criticize their actions in front of others, which may jeopardize married life.

INTEGRITY

Honesty in marriage is essential, it's like breathing in life. No marriage is perfect, mistakes are bound to happen by both partners, but simple apology and accepting the fault by keeping aside ego will resolve the differences and build a strong relationship.

Divorce is not the solution for marital stress, it is in repentance and forgiveness but not in separation. If there is complete trust and faith between husband and wife, it will never allow the seeds of doubt to grow in their relationship.

Integrity does not mean that one person surrenders to another blindly but has the courage to tell what is right and wrong and help in taking the person in the right direction.

VULNERABILITY

The influence of social media and technology has made all age groups of people vulnerable mentally and physically to an unimaginable range of products and services. Law of diminishing affects married couple also, its only matter of time, it may happen in few years or decades. To overcome the chances of becoming vulnerable both husband and wife need to speak to each other without having any filters and explore new avenues like going out on vacation etc., to keep their married life blissful. Children are the big catalyst who make husband and wife stay together even in tough times. History is proof that married men have also fallen prey to the beauty of a woman and there is no psychological reason to explain their action, the only antidote for this is wife.

OCCUPATION

Marriage and up brining of children require a well-trained mind, discipline, and character like any other occupational career. Women contribute more to marriage than men, because they must change their place of living, their method of work, even their name and changing their occupation after marriage, hence it's the responsibility of men to maintain that marriage works successfully.

Marriage is a full-time occupation, wherein a husband and wife should balance their professional jobs. Some conflicting careers between husband and wife can develop stress in their relation and unless both partners respect and understand each other's job responsibilities. Many types of job may require either partner to travel frequently or work late night with opposite sex colleagues, which again can create differences in married life unless both husband and wife are transparent in their work culture and ethics.

Sometimes one partner may be more successful in professional career, which should be appreciated by other instead of feeling jealous; especially men should keep away their ego and celebrate their wife's success. The choice of professional career should be discussed and agreed by wife and husband and should never become reason for divorce after marriage.

RELATIONSHIP

When a man and woman get married, they enter a new type of relationship which suppress all their previous relationships, but not necessarily disconnecting with the past. Parents and siblings will always be part of the extended family and both partners should never try to hurt each other family members. No spouse expects his or her husband or wife to show equal love to their family members, but never tolerate it if they are insulted in front of other people. Compared to men, women are more attached to their family members even after marriage and expect their husband to treat them well.

Relatives can be the real culprits for divorce, because they can never tolerate somebody being happier than them, hence never take the product of rumors mill seriously and doubt the integrity of your spouse.

Never doubt your spouse's relationship with friends, because the success of marriage stands on trust and faith, but sometimes this can be betrayed and in such a scenario both partners need to speak out the truth and find a remedy for the problem.

Relationships can be beautiful if both can accept anger and empathy along with hardship.

CHARACTER

Character of a person cannot be a reason for divorce after marriage, if it happens then either of the partners was not honest in disclosing their identity before marriage.

It's very difficult to change the character of a person, hence before getting married both the partners should do whatever is possible to understand each other and ensure their characters match as per their expectations. The old school thought that things get sorted out after marriage really do not work in the present generation, hence never take a hasty decision.

Love at first sight is like an accident, you never know the repercussions. Attraction at first sight is very common and people fall for it thinking of it as true love and pursuing the relationship without digging deep into a person's character just believing what the eyes see, and ears hear. You cannot judge a person by external behavior and the law of attraction blind folds the thought process which may result in not understanding the true character of a person and it can implode in future.

A person may change his attitude for some time but cannot hide his true character for a long time. When woman is credited for being behind every successful and unsuccessful man, there should not be reason why she cannot change the character of a person.

EGO

Ego and love cannot exist together. Apologizing does not mean you are wrong and other person is right, it just means you value relationships more than your ego.

Ego is the real villain behind every relationship break up or divorce. Marriage is between two people but not four, hence ditch the ego after marriage or else it will play with your partner and destroy your family into pieces.

Every good relationship is worthy of "Thank you" and "Sorry" never lose the gems of your life to the hidden Ego.

Conclusion: Marriage may be fixed in heaven, but it has to be been maintained and nurtured by both husband and wife. Differences exist everywhere which need to be sorted out but not separated. From birth till marriage a person undergoes a lot of physical and mental changes, but their parents never discard them, similarly after marriage a lot of changes do happen between couples, but they should never leave each other. Replacement rarely works in marriage; divorce is not a solution but a bigger problem which will push the person to isolation, forcing him to lead an unhappy and meaningless life.

Part C

69 i – Quotes

Every
marriage has
its own
problems,
what makes it
perfect is

if both partners
trust & support
each other
when things
go wrong

Be happy
not
because
everything
is good
but you
can see
good side of
everything

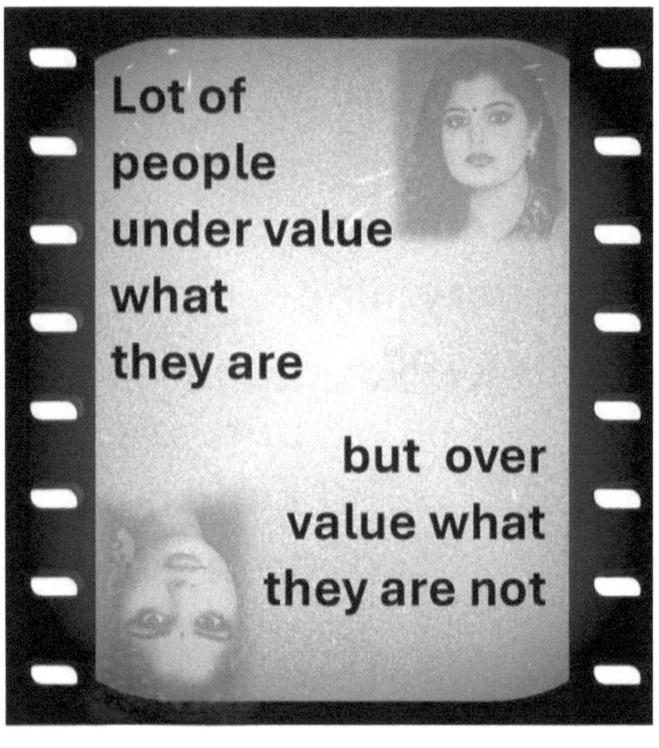

Lot of
people
under value
what
they are

but over
value what
they are not

When you
wish good
for others,
good things
come to
you.

That
is
law of
nature

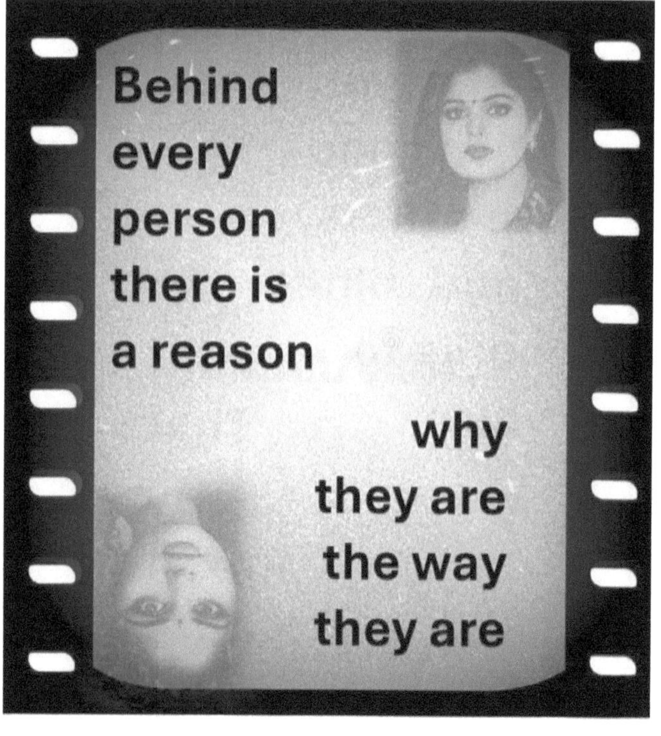
Behind
every
person
there is
a reason

why
they are
the way
they are

Your
belief
does not
change
reality
it can only
change how
you react
towards
reality

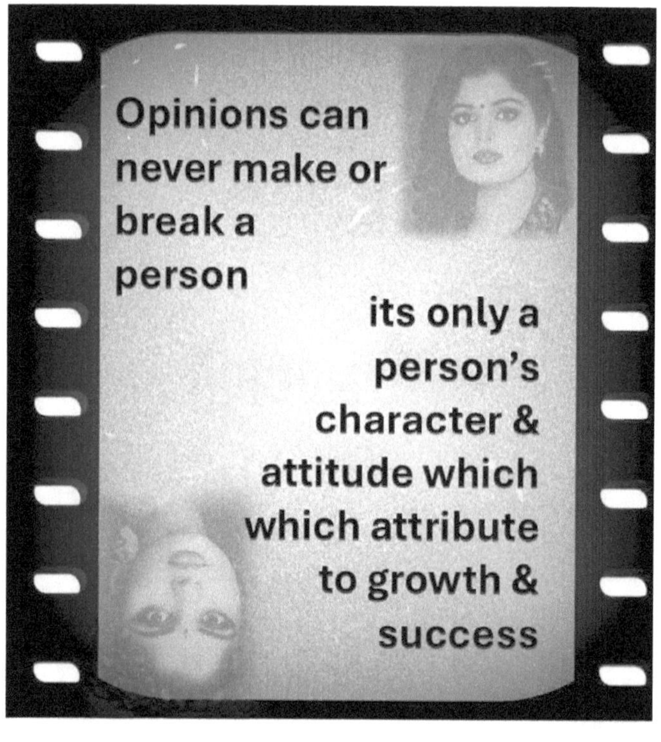
Opinions can
never make or
break a
person

its only a
person's
character &
attitude which
which attribute
to growth &
success

Worries &
tension are
like birds, we
cannot stop
them from
flying near us

but we can
stop them from
building a
nest in
our head

Bitter and
unhappy
people will
never trust
anyone
because
they don't see
good &
trust in
themselves

No family is
perfect, they
fight & even
stop talking
to each other

but at the end
family is family,
the love &
bonding will
never break

People who don't
value time
are the one who
keep crying
time is
not good
for them

Whatever
you do
good or
bad

some
people will
always make
negative
comments

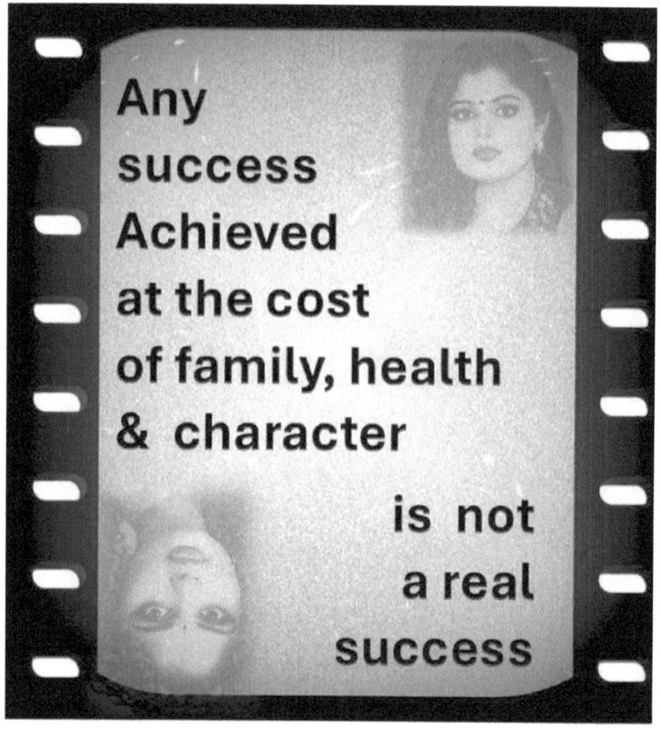
Any
success
Achieved
at the cost
of family, health
& character
is not
a real
success

Never
argue
with liars,
you
cannot win

because
they believe
in their lies

Successful
relationship
does not
depend on
each other
understandings,
it depends
on how well
they manage
their
misunderstanding

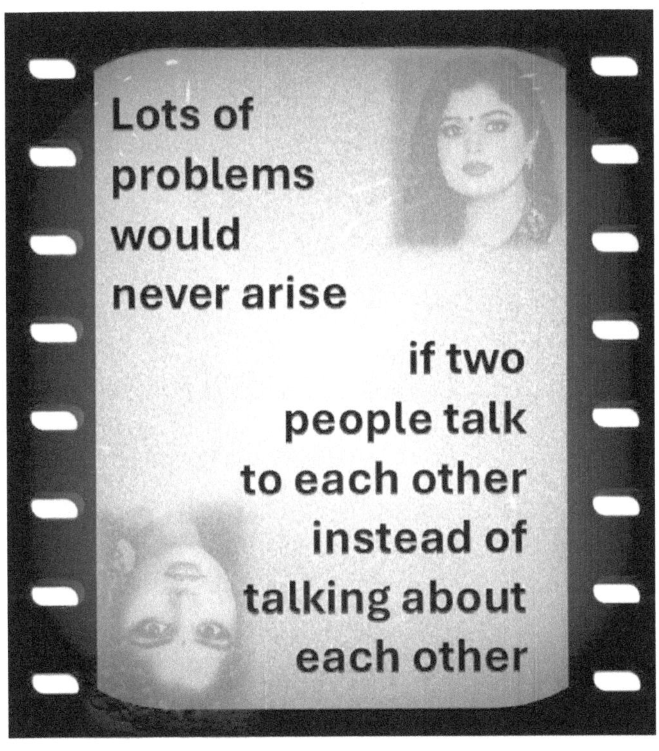
Lots of
problems
would
never arise
if two
people talk
to each other
instead of
talking about
each other

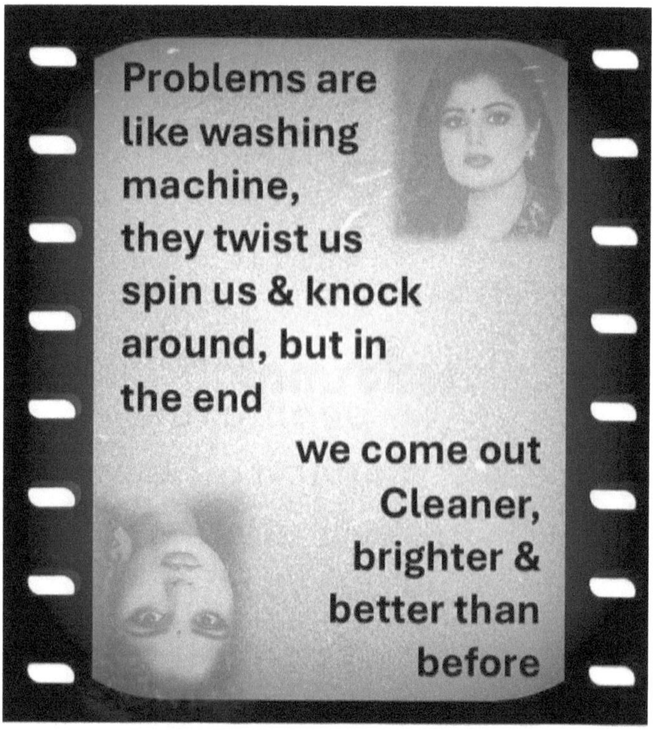
Problems are
like washing
machine,
they twist us
spin us & knock
around, but in
the end
we come out
Cleaner,
brighter &
better than
before

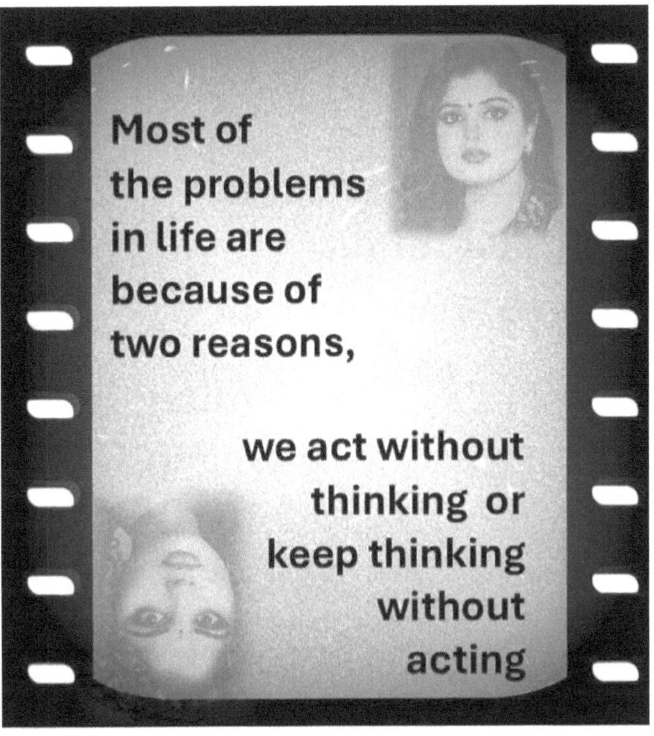

Most of
the problems
in life are
because of
two reasons,

we act without
thinking or
keep thinking
without
acting

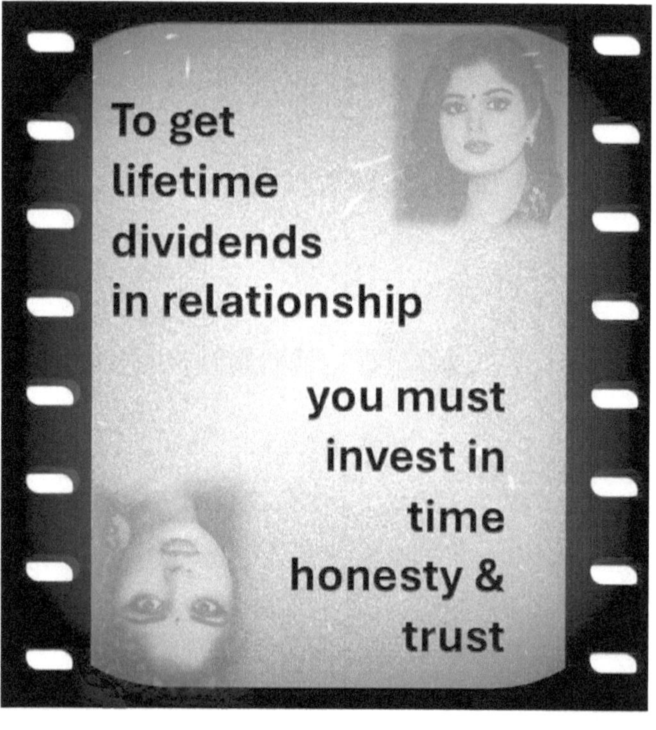
To get
lifetime
dividends
in relationship
you must
invest in
time
honesty &
trust

No
return on
investment
is profitable

if you have
to invest
your entire
life to earn
money

Parents spend
lot of money on
their children
education,

but rarely spend
little time
to teach them
how to live life.

Jealous
people
always
question the
good things, they
hear about others

but believe all the
bad things
without a
second
thought

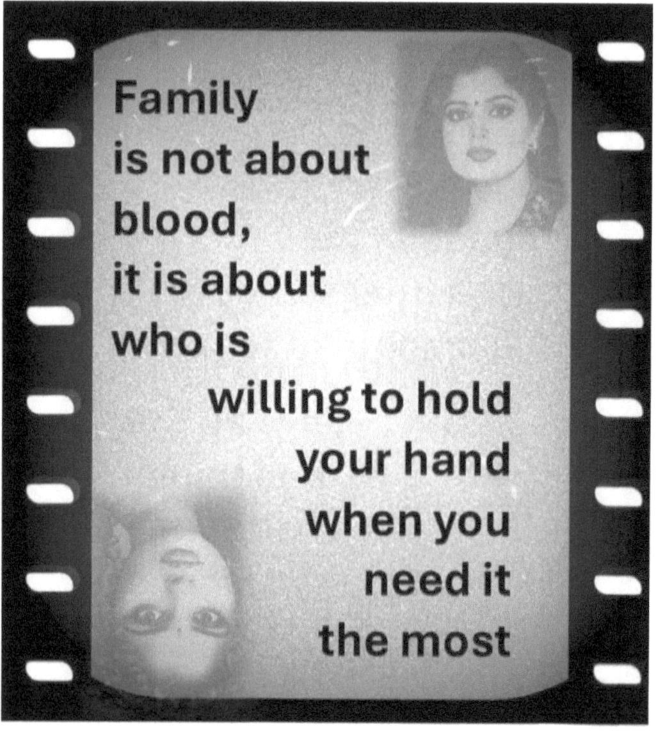
Family
is not about
blood,
it is about
who is
willing to hold
your hand
when you
need it
the most

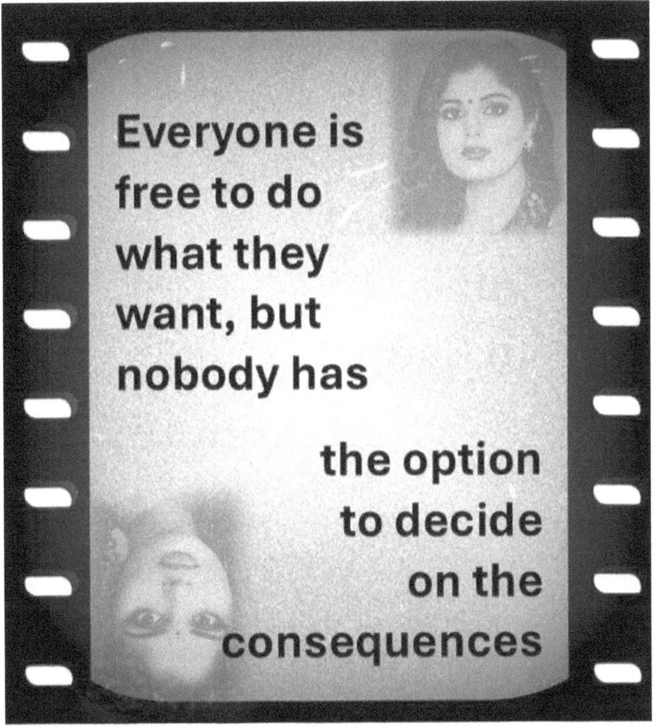
Everyone is
free to do
what they
want, but
nobody has
the option
to decide
on the
consequences

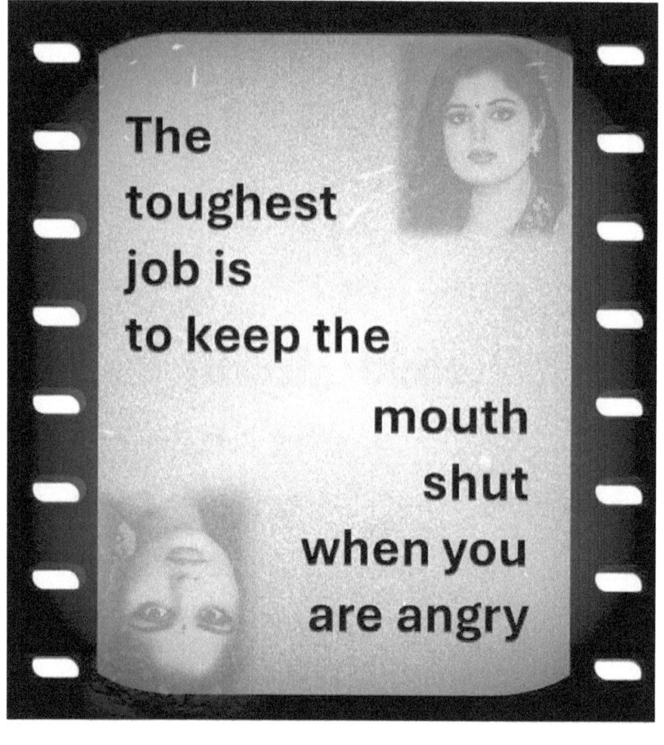
The
toughest
job is
to keep the
mouth
shut
when you
are angry

Feel
happy
for others
success

or else
jealousy
burns your
happiness

It is
important
to schedule
your priorities
but not
to prioritize
your
schedules

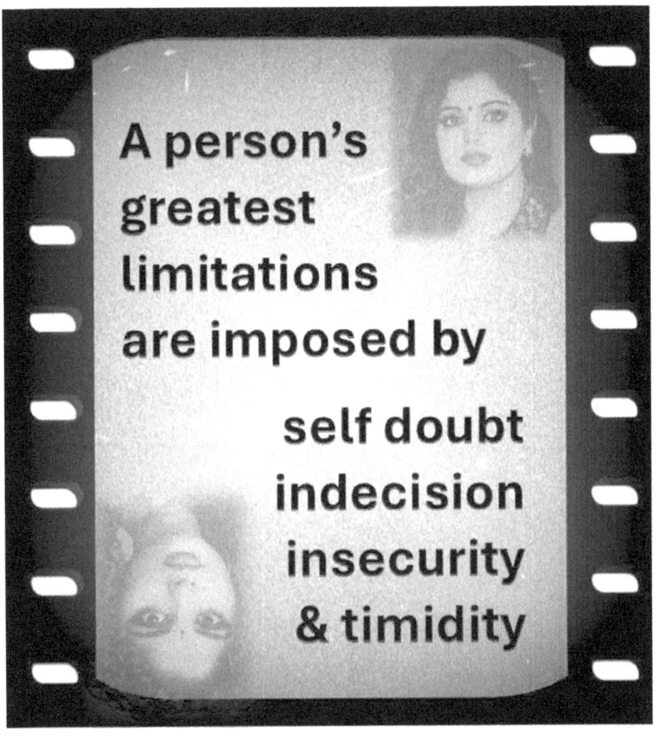
A person's
greatest
limitations
are imposed by
self doubt
indecision
insecurity
& timidity

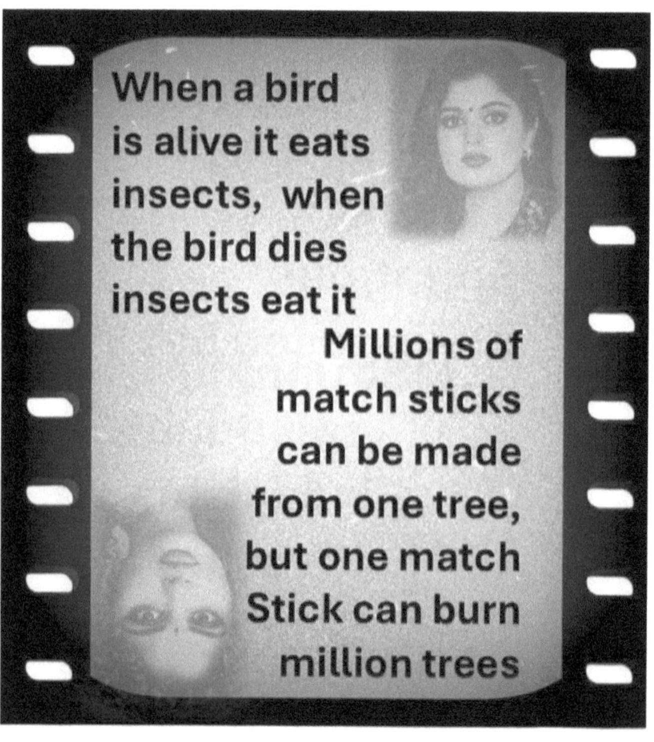
When a bird
is alive it eats
insects, when
the bird dies
insects eat it
Millions of
match sticks
can be made
from one tree,
but one match
Stick can burn
million trees

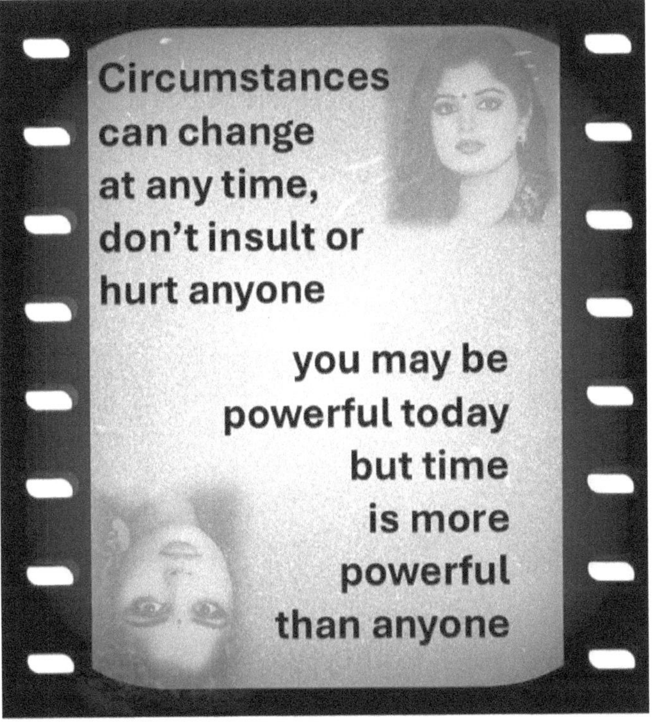
Circumstances
can change
at any time,
don't insult or
hurt anyone

you may be
powerful today
but time
is more
powerful
than anyone

Our destiny is not decided by GOD....
but written based on our actions
....even the small unnoticed action will be rewarded with bonus on maturity
But unfortunately we don't realize our mistakes & blame GOD for everything

Over
thinking
is the
biggest
cause
for
unhappiness

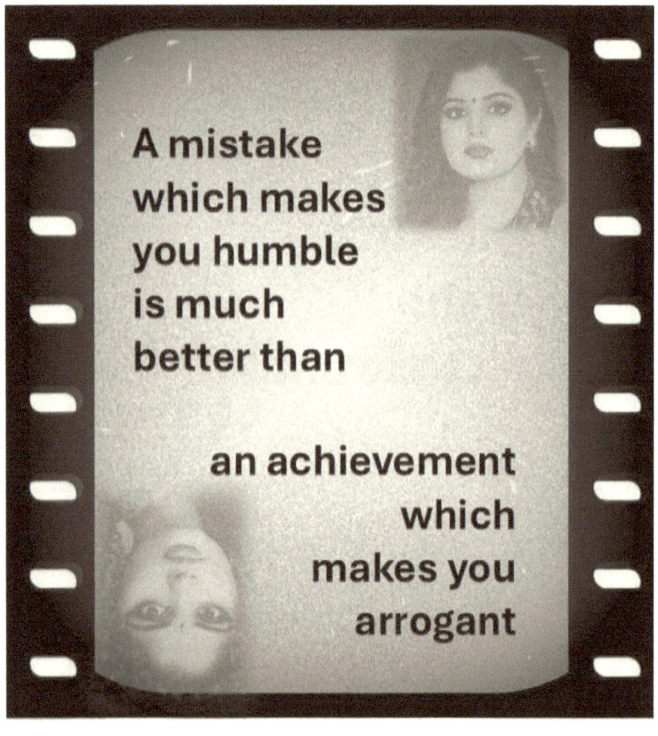
A mistake
which makes
you humble
is much
better than

an achievement
which
makes you
arrogant

Expectation
is the main
cause
for
unhappiness

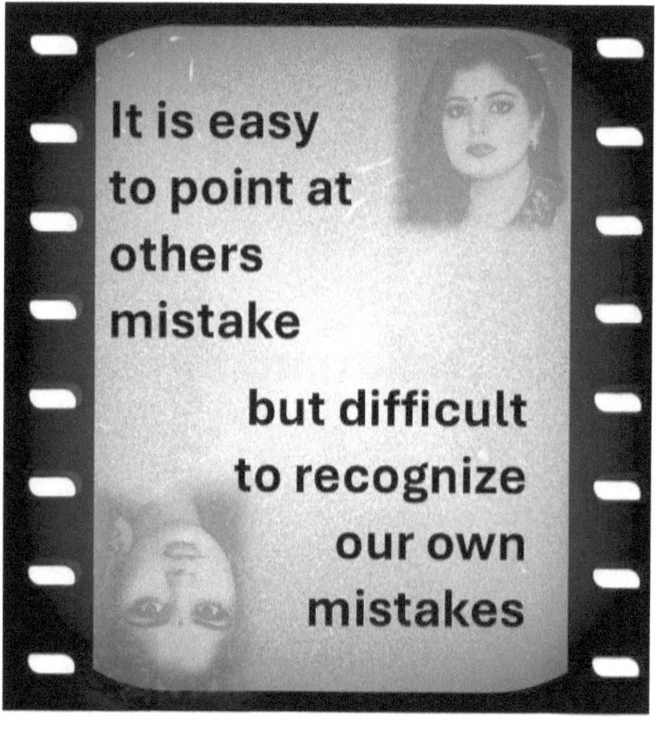
It is easy
to point at
others
mistake
but difficult
to recognize
our own
mistakes

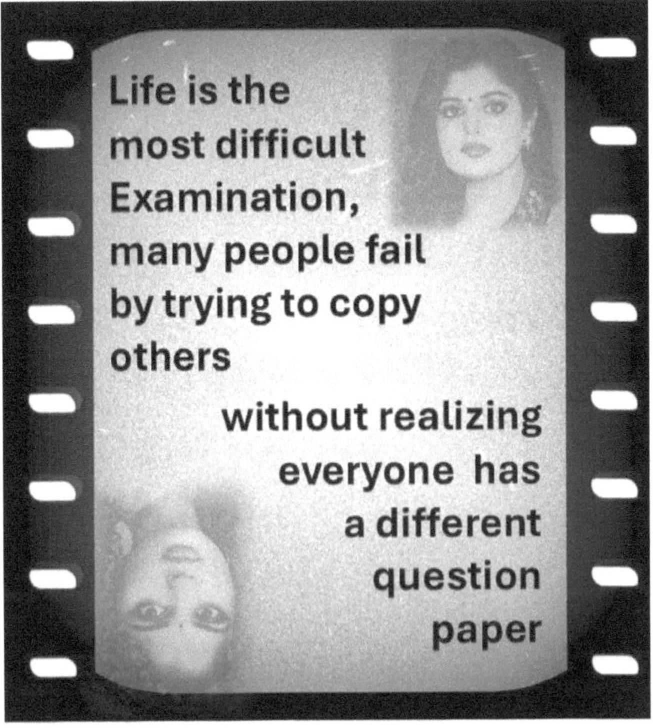
Life is the
most difficult
Examination,
many people fail
by trying to copy
others
without realizing
everyone has
a different
question
paper

Death is inevitable, but the image & character of the person remains forever

Life is a
colorful
journey,
don't
convert
into black
& white
with your
negative
thoughts

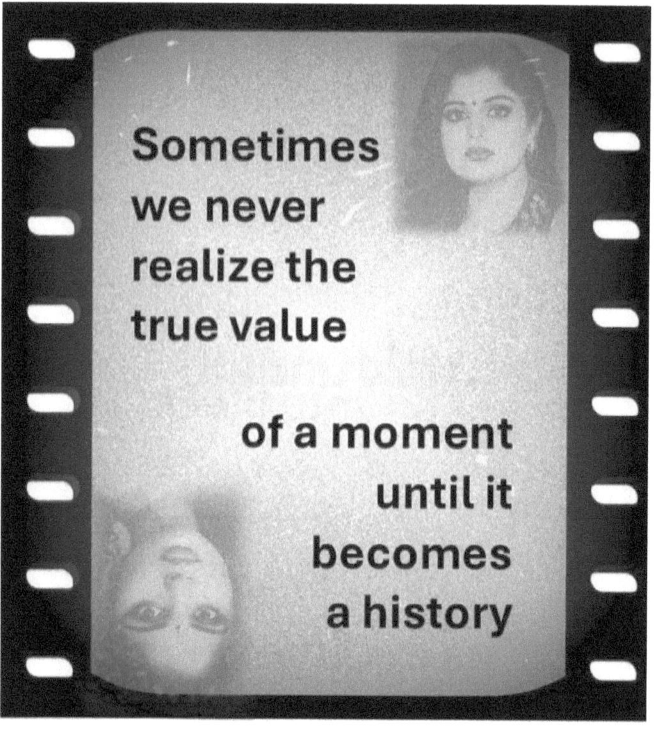
Sometimes
we never
realize the
true value

of a moment
until it
becomes
a history

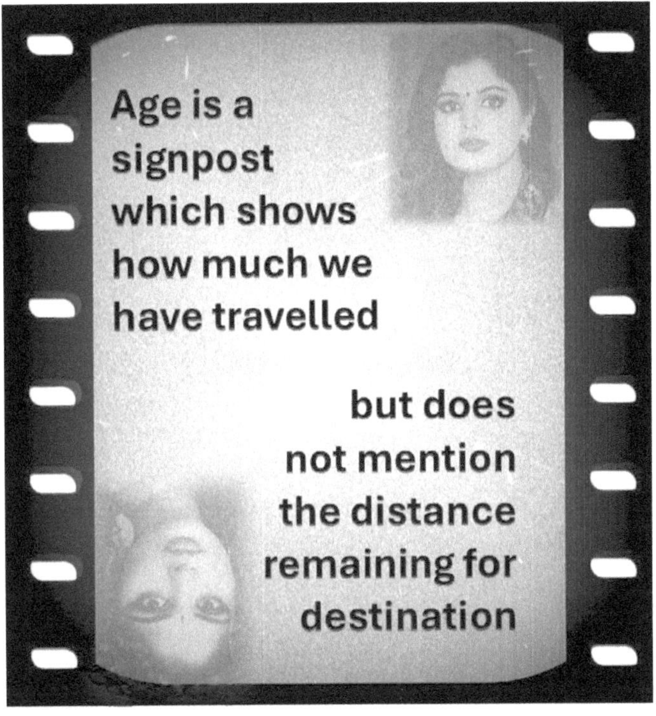
Age is a
signpost
which shows
how much we
have travelled

but does
not mention
the distance
remaining for
destination

People will never
understand somethings
until it happens to them

Life is very
unpredictable
make every day count
not for what you are, but what
you can do to preserve
our culture

Mobile
phone has
already
replaced
Camera, watch

alarm clock,
don't let
it replace
your
family

Don't allow
technology
to kill your
relationship
by giving
more time
& attention to
phone instead
of your partner

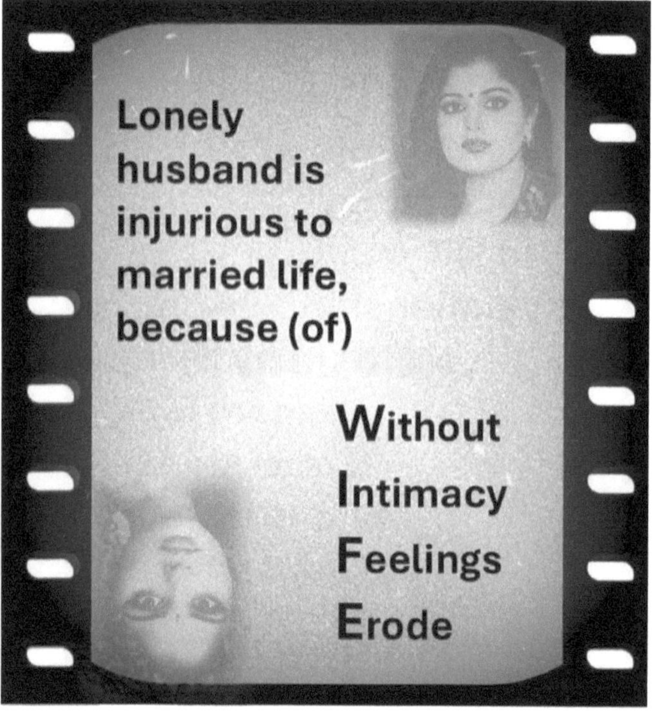
Lonely
husband is
injurious to
married life,
because (of)
Without
Intimacy
Feelings
Erode

Prosperity
does mean
filling your
locker with
Valuables, but
it's measured by
the amount of
happiness
you spread
within &
outside family

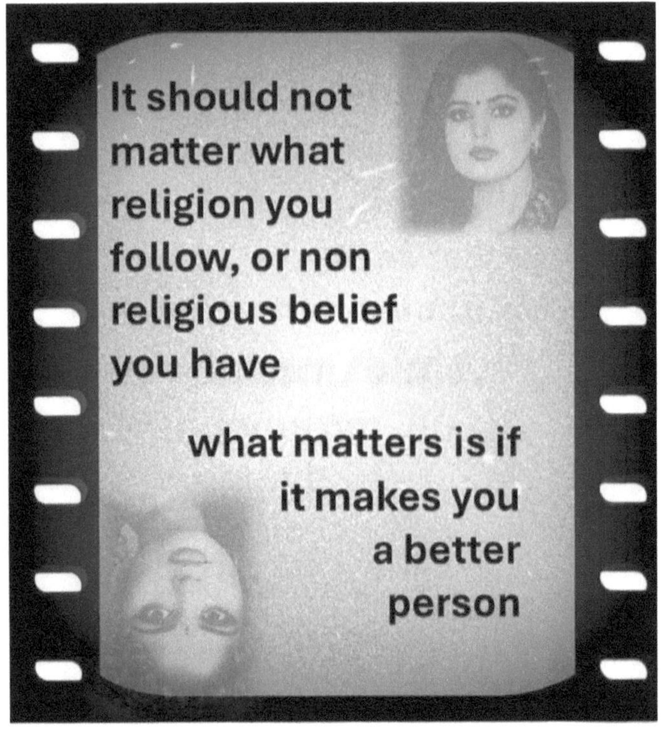
It should not matter what religion you follow, or non religious belief you have

what matters is if it makes you a better person

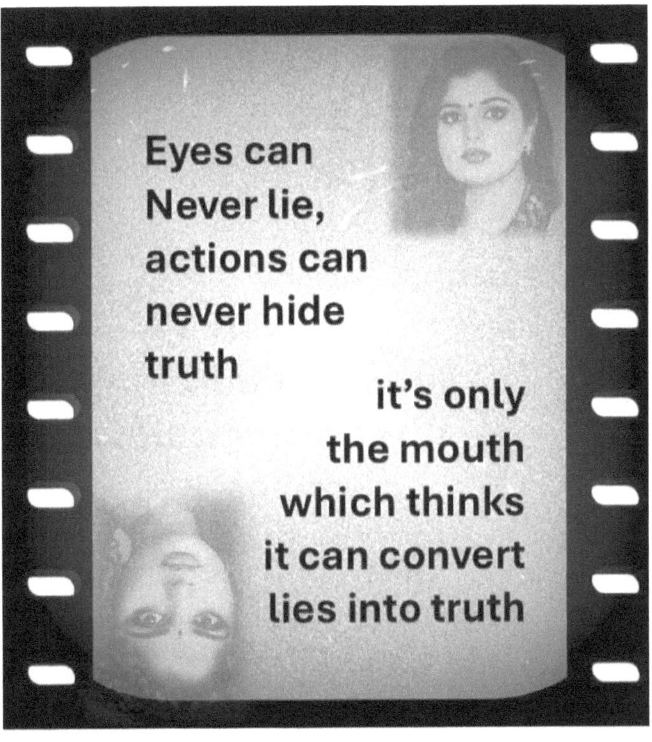
Eyes can
Never lie,
actions can
never hide
truth
it's only
the mouth
which thinks
it can convert
lies into truth

Problems are reactions of our past actions,
without introspection & rectifying our mistakes, we look for external solutions

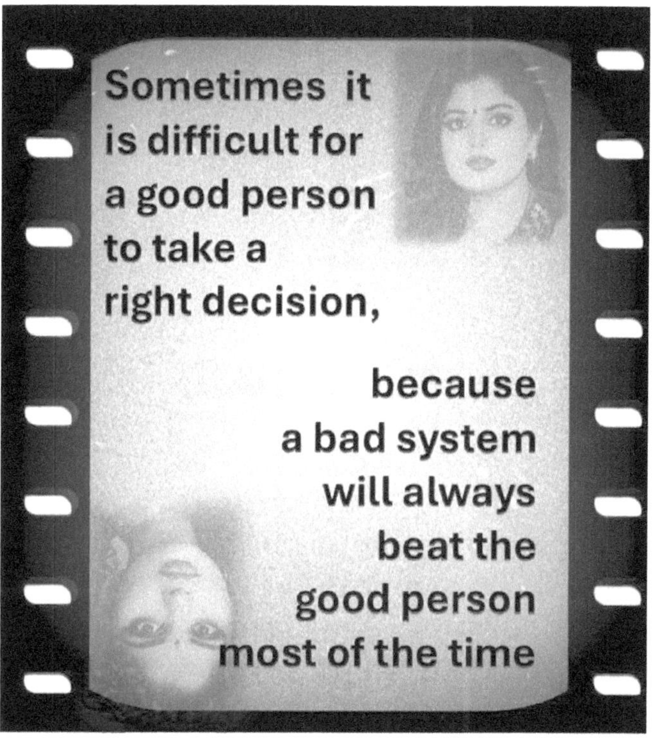

Sometimes it
is difficult for
a good person
to take a
right decision,

because
a bad system
will always
beat the
good person
most of the time

KARMA says
Don't abuse other people
it will increase their
lifetime, by reducing
from your quota.
Don't let your
precious lifetime
slip from your mouth

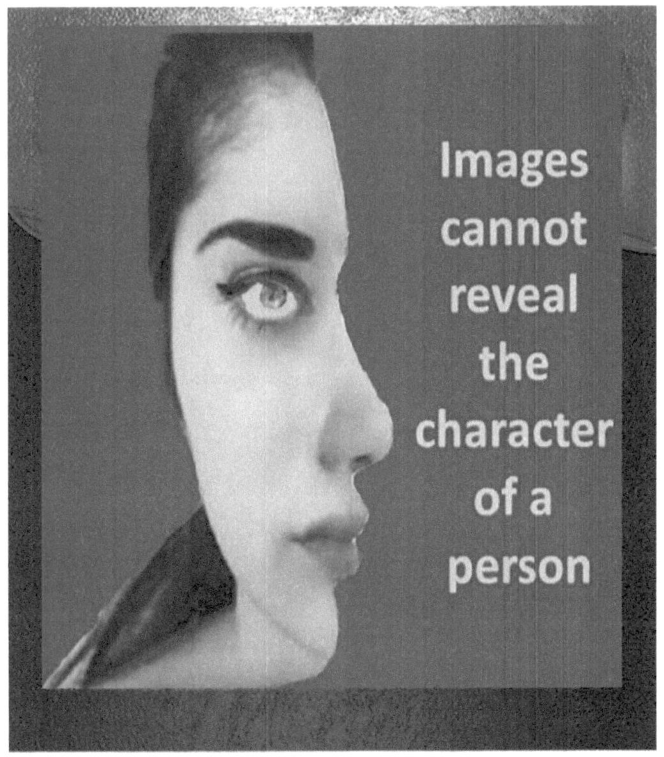
Images
cannot
reveal
the
character
of a
person

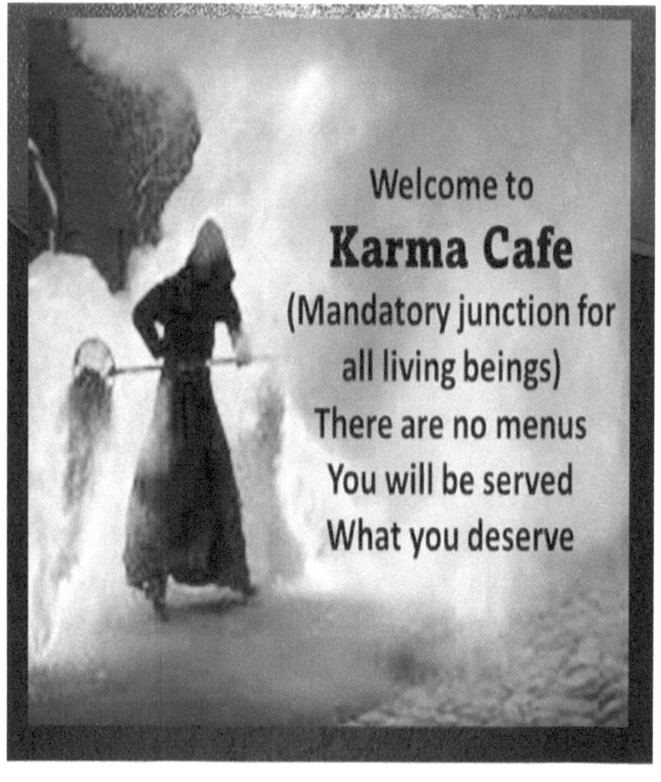
Welcome to
Karma Cafe
(Mandatory junction for
all living beings)
There are no menus
You will be served
What you deserve

If you
cannot
appreciate
others
good work

at least
don't
criticize
their efforts
& hard work

Reality hurts
more than truth

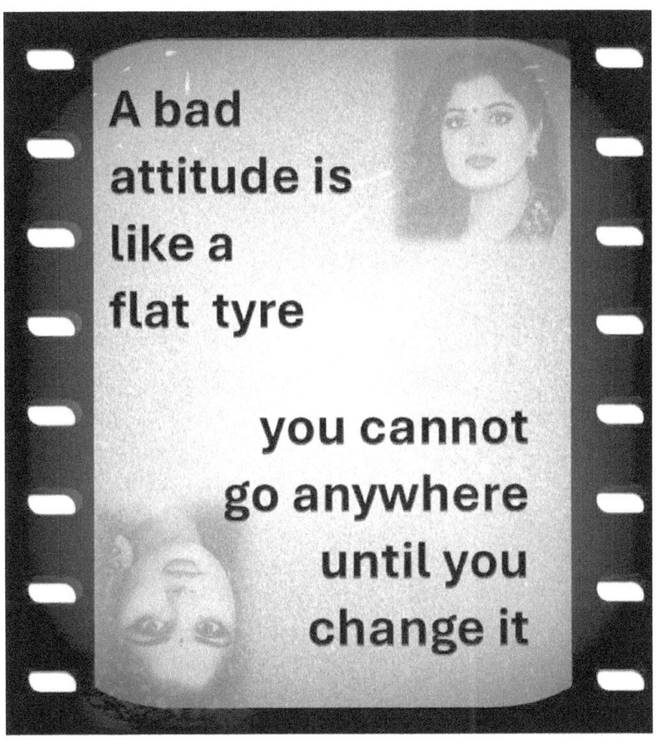

A bad
attitude is
like a
flat tyre

you cannot
go anywhere
until you
change it

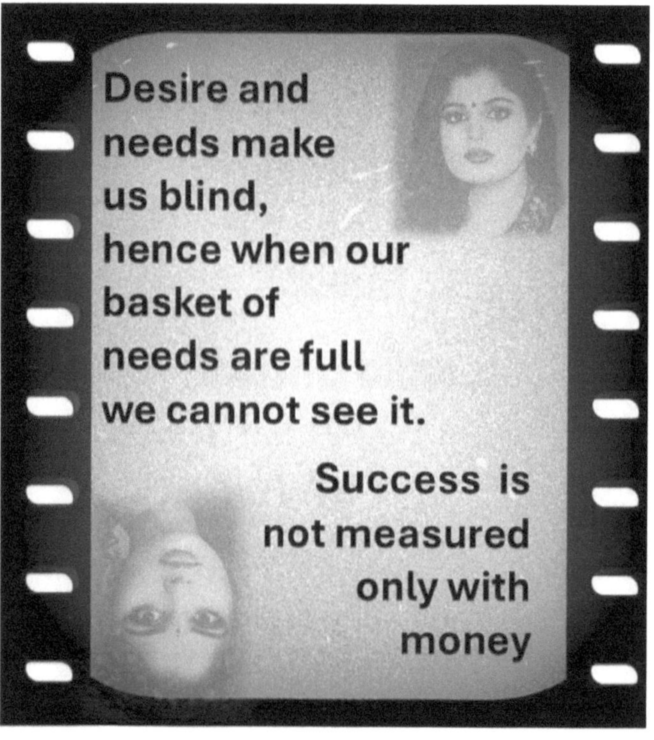

Desire and
needs make
us blind,
hence when our
basket of
needs are full
we cannot see it.

Success is
not measured
only with
money

I value
relationship
more than
my EGO
hence never
hesitate to
apologize
even when
I am not
wrong

S
B
K
G
H
Whatever happens
there is a reason, but
unfortunately we never
try to connect the dots,
to find the answer

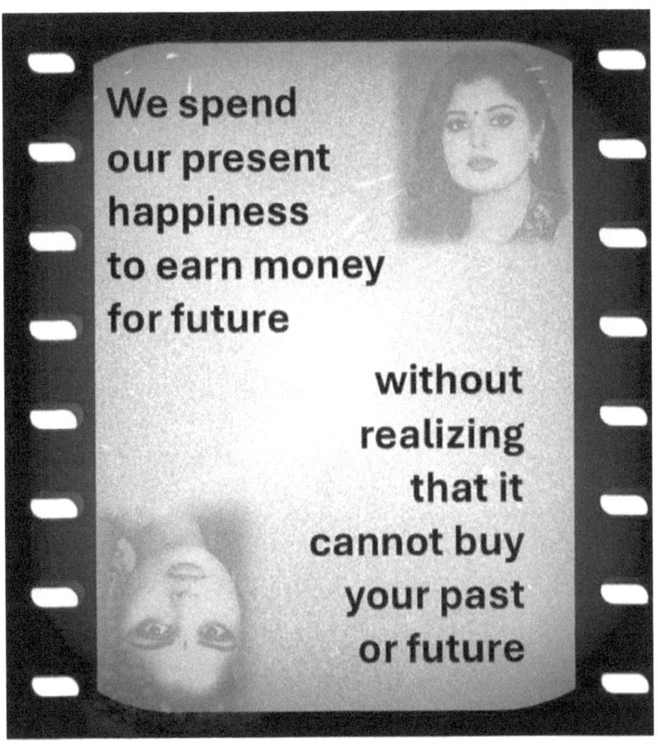
We spend
our present
happiness
to earn money
for future
without
realizing
that it
cannot buy
your past
or future

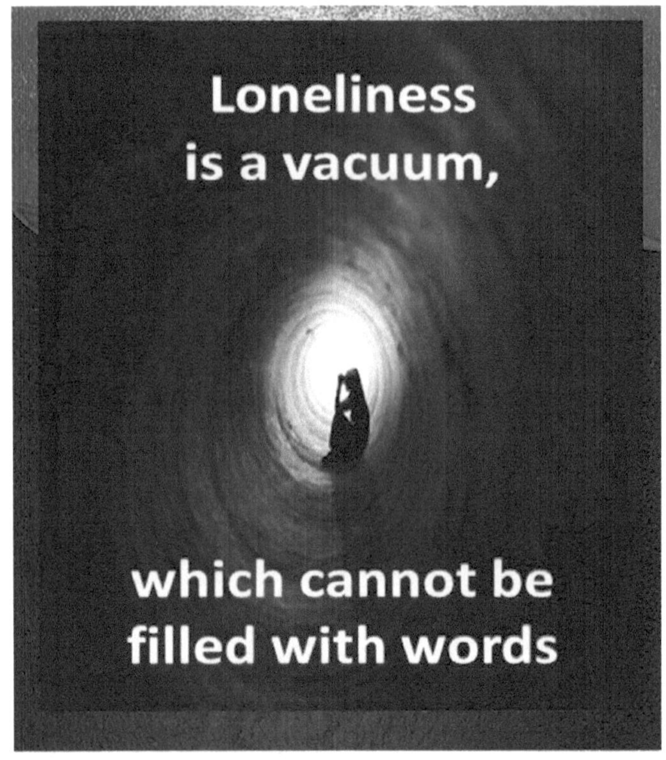
Loneliness
is a vacuum,
which cannot be
filled with words

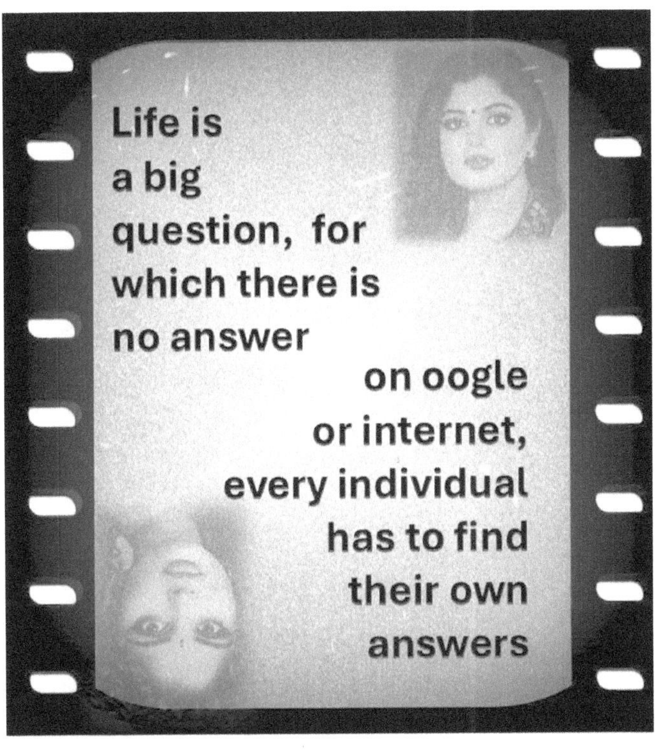
Life is
a big
question, for
which there is
no answer
on oogle
or internet,
every individual
has to find
their own
answers

Never hate
people who
are jealous
of you

because
they are
the ones
who think
you are better
than them

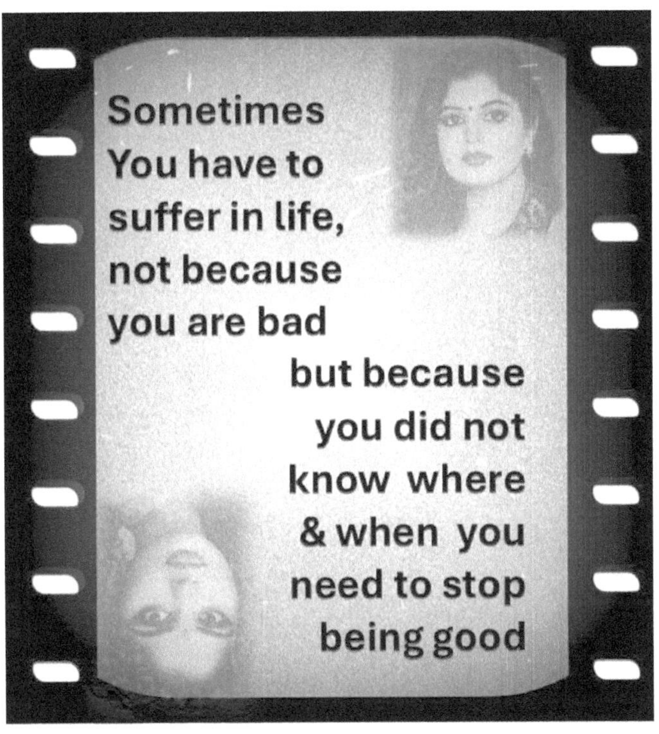
Sometimes
You have to
suffer in life,
not because
you are bad
but because
you did not
know where
& when you
need to stop
being good

The best thing about
worst time of your
life is that
you get to see the true
colors of everyone

Relationship is
like a bird in
hand, if you hold
tightly it will die,
if you hold
loosely it will fly,
but if you hold
with care it
remains with you
forever.

Beauty is illumination of soul

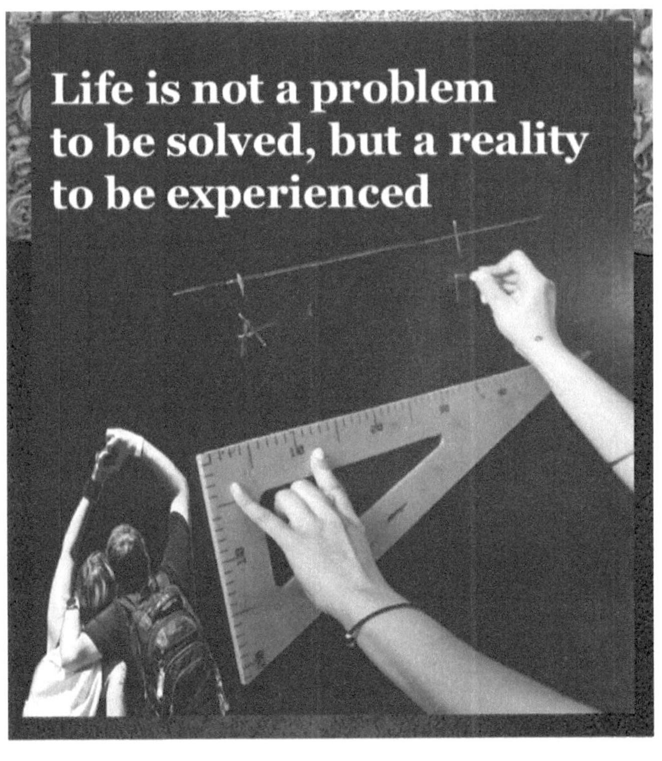
Life is not a problem
to be solved, but a reality
to be experienced

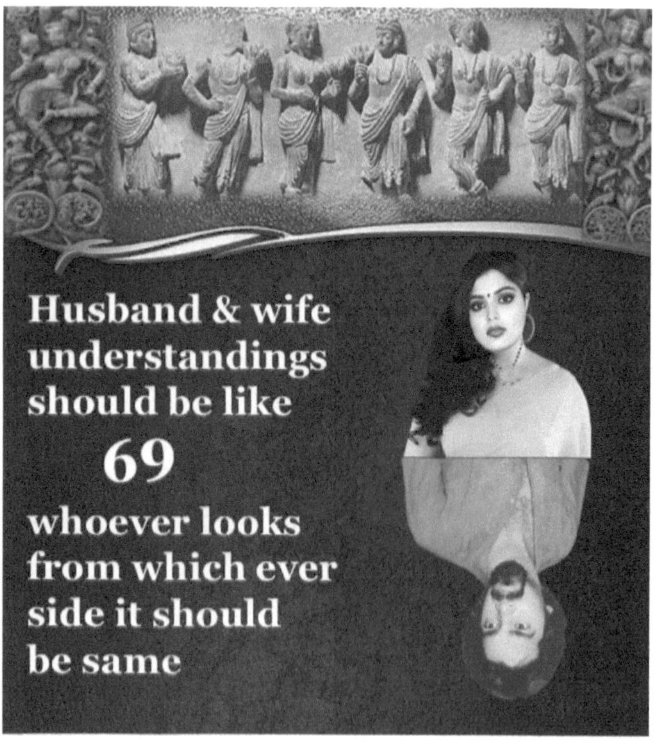
Husband & wife
understandings
should be like
69
whoever looks
from which ever
side it should
be same

www.ingramcontent.com/pod-product-compliance
Lightning Source LLC
Chambersburg PA
CBHW021227130726
47988CB00002B/854

9 798897 247868